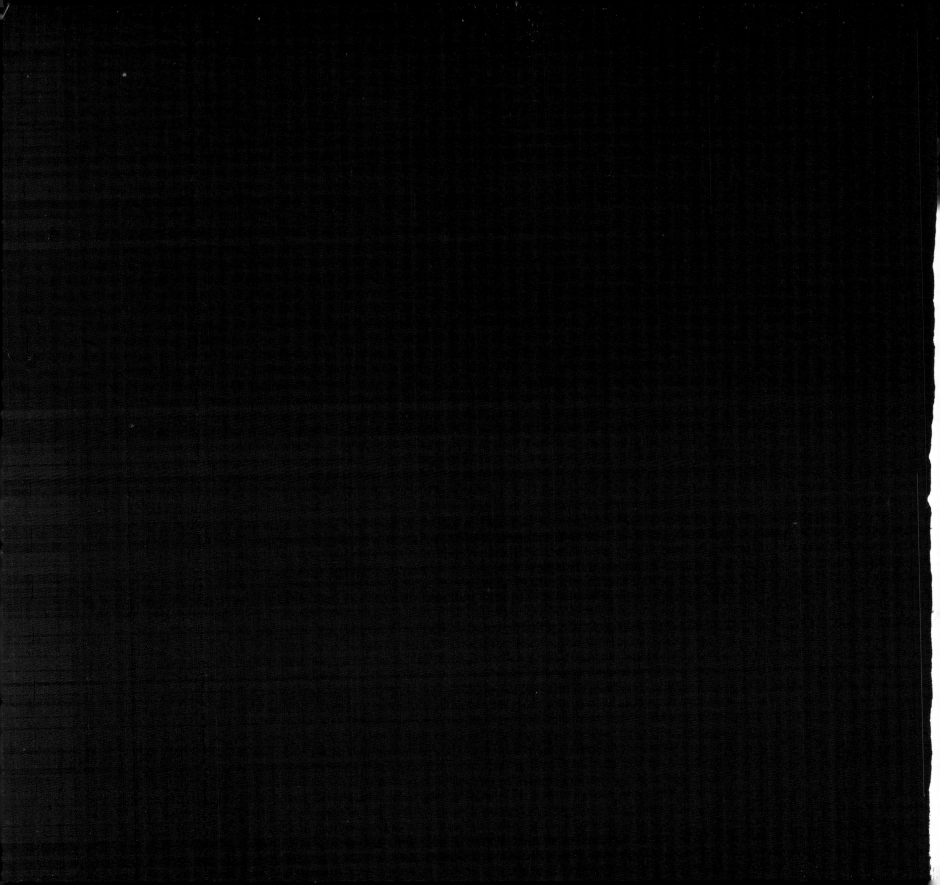

BECK

COWBOY VALUES

Recapturing What America Once Stood For

AUTHOR

JAMES P. OWEN

COLLABORATING WRITER

BRIGITTE LEBLANC

ART DIRECTOR / DESIGNER

NITA ALVAREZ

PHOTOGRAPHERS

MYRON BECK   DIANE CRISP   ROBERT DAWSON

WOUTER DERUYTTER   JAY DUSARD   MEHOSH DZIADZIO

CW GUILDNER   ROBB KENDRICK   DIANE LACY   BOB MOORHOUSE

GENE PEACH   KATHLEEN JO RYAN   LOUISE SERPA   BARBARA VAN CLEVE   JAMIE WILLIAMS

THE LYONS PRESS

GUILFORD, CONNECTICUT

AN IMPRINT OF THE GLOBE PEQUOT PRESS

The Lyons Press is an imprint of The Globe Pequot Press

Prepress by Apple Graphics Inc., Los Angeles, California, USA

Library of Congress Cataloging-in-Publication Data

Owen, James P.

  Cowboy values : recapturing what America once stood for / James P. Owen ; contributing writer, Brigitte Leblanc. — 1st ed.

  p. cm.

ISBN 978-1-59921-271-5

1. Conduct of life. 2. Values. I. Leblanc, Brigitte. II. Title.

BJ1581.2.094 2008

170.973—dc22   2007049964

Printed in China

10 9 8 7 6 5 4 3 2 1

To order additional copies of COWBOY VALUES, please visit **www.GlobePequot.com** or www.amazon.com.

To buy books in quantity for corporate use or incentives, call **(800) 962-0973** or email **premiums@GlobePequot.com.**

To

STANYA

from whom I've learned so much

about life...about love...

about heart....

America is great because she is good.
If America ceases to be good,
America will cease to be great.

attributed to **ALEXIS DE TOCQUEVILLE** 1805-1859

IN THE LAST HALF-CENTURY, America has gone through the Swinging Sixties, the Me Decade, the PC revolution, the rise of globalization, and the dawn of the Internet Age. So what about the decade ahead? Years hence, how will social historians characterize the times we're entering right now?

My take on that question might surprise you. Though I began writing this book discouraged by the state of our country, I finished it with a feeling of hope. I'm betting that future scholars will see the next few years as a time when America finally got back on track.

How can I be so upbeat when our society seems to be falling around our ears? It's true that if I went solely by what I see on the 24-hour news networks and in other mainstream media, I'd be convinced our country is in an irreversible downward slide. But I have a different vantage point.

Having been on the speaking circuit since my last book, *Cowboy Ethics*, was published in late 2004, I've had the chance to talk with hundreds of people ~ all kinds of people ~ about where our country is headed. I've heard from so many who are sick and tired of a culture that glorifies materialism and self-gratification. They are disheartened by the breakdown of ideals and institutions Americans once revered. Above all, they are hungry for a sense of meaning and connection in their lives.

For some years now, the unspoken rule in our country has been "every man for himself." With globalization spreading uncertainty, Americans have been operating as if we're in a massive game of musical chairs ~ one where you do whatever it takes to survive and come out on top. When we see corporate executives bilking shareholders because the millions they already have just aren't enough ~ well, it shows how far the excesses can go.

I believe the pendulum is now poised to swing the other way. Our leaders may not get it, but at the grassroots level a lot of Americans realize we're all in this together. They know that if we don't stand united, we should be prepared to fall individually.

Intuitively, many people also understand that the future of our society depends on the values we hold dear. Are we more concerned about what happened to Anna Nicole Smith or what's happened to the survivors of Hurricane Katrina? Do we measure someone by the kind of character their actions reveal? Or by the kind of car they drive? We have to decide what really matters to us or risk seeing the foundations of our country crumble.

COWBOY MORE THAN EVER

What's more, if we want to solve the formidable problems we face, we can't sit back and wait for the government or someone else to do it. We need to rally around the ideals our nation is built upon ~ values we can all believe in ~ like courage, optimism, and self-reliance.

That is why I'm convinced it's time for the cowboy to regain his place as a leading American icon. To the young people of my generation, cowboys were heroes to be admired and emulated. They were the good guys who stood up for what was right, no matter how great the dangers. Our matinee idols might have been fictional characters, but in truth, they were just larger-than-life versions of real people from our history ~ the cowboys whose code of honor and hard work helped civilize the West. Where does this generation find role models like that?

In today's America, the role of *character* in living a good life is usually unstated and too often overlooked. It's always been assumed that your family and your community would instill the time-honored values upon which this country was built. But as we see those bedrock values being overwritten by a consumer and media-centered culture, it's clear we can no longer take them for granted.

The cowboy way of life couldn't be more different. It's a culture in which character counts above all. Even today, being a cowboy isn't a job description. It's a position of respect that must be earned. You might be able to ride and rope with the best of them. But if your actions don't bespeak a strong sense of honor, you're not a real cowboy and you'll never be accepted as part of the cowboy community.

The reason America needs the cowboy is simple. Cowboys stand for something ~ which means they have a clear, unshakable set of beliefs they live by each day. Based on what I've heard from people across the country, most Americans *want* to believe in something. We are seeking a solid core to anchor our lives.

The cowboy is not only a symbol of what's best about America, but a living example of it. Though the open range is long gone, the Cowboy Way is still alive and well across America, as the photos in this book so richly demonstrate.

I believe it's not too late for America to recapture the qualities that made us a great nation. Like the cowboy, they are still here. We just need to be reminded of them. And that's what this book is all about.

Jim Owen

JAMES P. OWEN
Austin, Texas

*What
America
has lost*

DAWSON

ARE OUR BEST DAYS BEHIND US?

THIS IS THE BOOK I wish I didn't have to write. But I feel I have no choice. I can't just stand by and watch as the best things about America slip into our past.

My last book, *Cowboy Ethics*, grew from my disgust over corporate wrongdoing on Wall Street, where I spent more than 40 years of my career. Those feelings now have escalated to outrage and alarm over the state of our society at large. Can any thinking American today believe our country isn't seriously off-track?

Symptoms of a spreading malaise surround us. Through the lens of 24/7 media feeds, we see a rash of ethical scandals spreading across business, government, and even the church. A materialistic, media-driven culture focused on celebrity and wealth. Policies that only widen the gap between haves and have-nots. And a willingness to sacrifice long-term well-being for the sake of short-term payoffs in government and the private sector alike.

What does it say about our society when nearly two-thirds of young adults say that getting rich is the most important goal in life? It's distressing enough when 75 percent of high school students admit they've cheated to get better grades. Worse still, half the students say they see nothing wrong with it.

What does it say about our business ethos when corporate executives can ride around in limos and corporate jets while axing thousands of jobs in the name of shareholder value? I'm as big a believer in free enterprise as anyone. But belief in our economic system is being undercut by greedy executives and Gordon Gekko wannabes who let the profit motive run amok.

This American system of ours...
call it Americanism, call it capitalism,
call it what you will...gives each and
every one of us a great opportunity
if we only seize it with both hands
and make the most of it.

AL CAPONE

And what does it say about our system of government when Congress seems too bound by partisan politics ~ or too beholden to special interests ~ to get the real work done? Our lawmakers seem powerless to fix Social Security, tackle our health care crisis, resolve the immigration debate, or take meaningful steps on issues of energy independence and climate change.

This is hardly a partisan view. Citizens of all political stripes have reasons to decry the state of the union. Conservative hackles are raised by the huge deficits, rampant pork-barrel spending, and a "pay to play" mentality. Liberals are incensed by ongoing assaults on the middle class, brazen corporate greed, and gaping holes in the social service safety net. Libertarians fret over the erosion of civil liberties and personal responsibility. Even setting aside the mess in Iraq, there is plenty of outrage to go around.

Public opinion polls, those mood rings of our society, tell a story of deepening pessimism among our populace. Currently only one in five Americans believes our nation is going in the right direction. Of those who think we're heading the wrong way, some 80 percent think our direction is symptomatic of a longer-term decline. Equally telling, nearly two-thirds of Americans think their children's lives will be worse than theirs. Although the U.S. economy continues to grow, for many the vision of America as a land of opportunity and upward mobility has faded.

Once we were admired around the globe as the defender of freedom and foe of injustice. Now we are widely regarded as an arrogant, self-important bully operating with few principles other than an implicit belief that our economic and military might makes us right. With the Abu Ghraib and Guantanamo debacles, America's world standing has sunk to an all-time low. Through our actions, we have squandered the support and sympathy the world community showered on us in the wake of 9/11.

Even among our European and Asian allies, the U.S. is increasingly seen as a disruptive and dangerous force in the world. In years past, citizens of other nations tended to look more favorably on the American people than on our institutions or leaders. But that distinction no longer holds true, as documented by the Pew Research Center. Its recent survey found that in Canada, the Netherlands, and France, as well as in Turkey and Pakistan, a majority see ordinary American citizens as greedy or violent. Now we are reviled not just for what our country does, but for who we are.

Historically, the world has always given us the benefit of the doubt because it believed we meant well. It no longer does.

BRENT SCOWCROFT
National Security Adviser to Presidents Gerald Ford and George H.W. Bush

A Hard Look in the Mirror

One thing I know for sure: This is *not* the America I grew up with. And that's not based on some nostalgic, picture-postcard view of our past. From the days of Wounded Knee to Jim Crow to the McCarthy witch hunts to Watergate, our country has always had its dark underbelly. History makes it painfully clear we haven't always been on the side of right.

Even so, we aspired to live up to a higher standard. We still thought of America, without irony, as the land of the free and the home of the brave. We were the country that sacrificed to defend our allies, helped our former enemies to rebuild, and opened welcoming arms to the refugees of the world. Weren't we the ones who believed in justice and fair play? Weren't we the people admired around the world for being honest, hard-working, optimistic, and generous? That's certainly the image invoked whenever the Fourth of July rolls around.

But somewhere along the line, something fundamental to our national character has shifted. In the America I knew, those who lied, cheated, or broke the law were considered to be the bad apples ~ people to be shunned and treated as outcasts. These days, anything less than a sensational scandal or a capital crime raises little more than a blip on our moral radar screens.

Is anyone really surprised when a high public official is accused of corruption? Are we shocked that corporate executives would back-date stock options? How many of us believe that professional athletes "just say no" to performance-enhancing drugs? Where's the outrage? Where's the shame?

We used to believe that playing by the rules ~ showing up on time, doing your job to the best of your ability ~ was the surest way to get ahead in America. Now, watching Wall Street titans make their gazillions while ordinary middle-class households lose ground, it's harder to see things that way.

DAWSON

The strong idealistic streak running through the American psyche has given way to a deep, pervasive cynicism. No wonder Americans express such a lack of faith in our institutions and even less trust in our leaders. We've come to expect the worst, and too often get it. Along the way, we seem to have lost the belief in our own goodness. It's as though Mr. Smith went to Washington and ended up working for a ring of identity thieves.

We can't help being aware of our lowered expectations, because more and more they filter into our daily lives. At what point did it become common for seemingly upstanding commuters to give other drivers the finger? When did first-graders stop saying "yes, ma'am" and start using the f-word? Nobody wants to return to the days of uptight, Victorian repression. But you don't have to be Miss Manners to lament the decline of civility in American life.

While the fine points of our social compact were being rewritten, so were our standards of discourse. What once would have been labeled yellow journalism is now mainstream headline news.

In media terms, one juicy celebrity item is worth more than a dozen serious news stories, especially if it involves household names behaving badly. We're in the midst of Culture Wars, and the "girls gone wild" crowd seems to be winning. Can latter-day gladiators be far behind?

Bad manners and tabloid-style journalism may not be all that important in the big scheme of things. But I think they reflect a general slide into a crasser, more narcissistic mode of operating that *is* undermining larger American ideals. Arrogance toward voters, employees, or shareholders stems from the same mindset that leads to arrogant foreign policy. Trampling on a neighbor's flowers is not that distant from trampling on others' rights.

One of America's strengths has always been a willingness to look in the mirror, even if the image is disturbing. This is one reason we're able to celebrate progress in overcoming injustices ranging from slavery to racial discrimination to denial of women's rights. So if we take a hard look in the glass today, what do we see?

What does America stand for now?

In the eyes of many around the world, friend and foe alike, America is a glutton ~ a society with an insatiable appetite for consumption stoked by an endless flow of goods from Asian factories. Economists tell us that a large share of the productivity gains we've achieved through technology have gone overseas so American consumers can accumulate closets full of inexpensive electronics, clothes, and toys.

A man who doesn't stand for

something will fall

for anything.

DAWSON

Meanwhile, our biggest export is a mass-marketed, media-driven culture celebrating material wealth, youth, and celebrity. Our country ceaselessly promotes democracy and free enterprise abroad while sweeping under the rug the apathy and inequities at home.

It's no wonder that on the world stage, we come off as an overbearing, sanctimonious *über*-superpower convinced that our military and economic might makes us right. The U.S. once held the moral high ground, but we can't credibly claim it anymore.

We've become the spoiled brats in the family of man.

Might does not make right.

Right makes might.

I know I'm not alone in believing the American way of life has taken a seriously wrong turn. And the concerns run far deeper than who is in the White House. Since my book, *Cowboy Ethics*, was published in late 2004, I've traveled extensively throughout our country, speaking to groups of all sizes. Along the way, I've heard reactions from hundreds of people from all walks of life who share the same uneasiness. In spite of our many comforts and financial success, we can't shake the feeling that something is amiss at the very core of our lives. Worse still, we have no idea how to fix it.

Terrorism may not be the biggest danger we face. Once we see ourselves on a downward spiral and feel powerless to change it, we are at risk of losing heart. When our nation's long-cherished ideals start to ring hollow, we begin losing touch with our collective soul. And if we shrug and say, "It is what it is," we've already given up hope for the next generation.

DAWSON

How Did We Get Here?

The state of our country is disquieting, to say the least, and we can't help looking for something or someone to blame; that's human nature. What's more, we've got a long list of culprits to point to, depending on our varying points of view.

Some see sensationalized media content, violent video games, and gangsta rap as the prime sources of pernicious influence. Others point to rising poverty, high divorce rates, or families that don't eat dinner together. To some conservatives, our problems are rooted in the counterculture of the 1960s, while liberals might lay them at the feet of big business or the military-industrial complex. Do our troubles stem from taking religion out of our schools? Or lax parenting? Or a generation of Baby Boomers who had it too easy?

Americans have always been able to handle austerity and even adversity. Prosperity is what is doing us in.

JAMES RESTON

Personally, I think each of these answers might hold a grain of truth ~ and all are skirting the real story. Yes, we've seen swift, radical changes in our way of life. High schools didn't used to be equipped with metal detectors. Our parents didn't have to worry about pedophiles trolling the Internet. And workers used to believe they could at least count on Social Security, if not a pension, after a lifetime of work. But I think the fault lines in our culture run deeper than that.

To my mind, what's happened since World War II is a fundamental shifting and splintering of values throughout the layers of American society. I saw how dramatic this change has been several months ago when I addressed students and faculty at the graduate business school of a large public university in the Midwest. When I invited questions at the end of my talk, an earnest-looking young man raised his hand. He hesitated just a second before asking, "Mr. Owen, do you think it's possible to succeed in business today and still be ethical?"

I was so astonished, I hardly knew what to say. Here was clearly a bright, thoughtful student who spent his days studying accounting methods, quantitative analysis, and strategic thinking. He was about to graduate from a highly regarded program designed to train the next generation of business leaders. And he would be entering the work world uncertain how he could square ambition with principles ~ or whether it could even be done.

Thinking back to my own business school classes, I honestly don't believe the idea of an inherent conflict between being a good person and doing well in business would even have occurred to us. I didn't know whether to be glad he was thinking about the ethical dimensions of his chosen profession, or completely discouraged that a young man would feel so cynical about a career he hadn't even launched yet. I couldn't help wondering what lessons young people are taking from us and the world we have left them.

In Pursuit of the Good Life

One lesson has come through loud and clear: You'd better get rich or you're screwed.

My father's generation believed that if you were smart, hardworking, and kept your nose clean (whatever that meant), you'd earn enough for you and your family to live a comfortable life. But for a lot of people today, that's not enough. They want to get as much as they can, as fast as they can, however they can.

What changed? The dynamics of the stock market, for one thing. With the boom of the Nineties, we saw day-traders making far more on stock flips than they could ever earn in their regular jobs. Then, along came the young dot-com entrepreneurs ~ some of them mega-millionaires before they were eligible to vote. Becoming fabulously wealthy was no longer a pipe dream; it was dangling right in front of our eyes, there for the taking.

Greed became respectable.

Vast wealth and all the fun you could have with it was a theme the media could really run with. Instead of the modest postwar bonanzas of "Queen for a Day" ~ deserving Moms win the labor-saving appliances their families could never quite afford ~ we had "Lifestyles of the Rich and Famous" showing us how to spend money more lavishly than even Elvis could have imagined. It has been a straight line to the wretched excesses of "The Real Housewives of Orange County."

Even if you couldn't be one of the rich and famous, you could still emulate their style of living large with a little help from advertising, glossy magazines, and an explosion of low-priced goods from Asia. "Affordable luxury" became the catchphrase linking everything from 500-thread-count sheets to five-dollar lattés.

Home is where you keep your stuff while you are out buying more stuff.

GEORGE CARLIN

So what's so bad about all this? Surely there's nothing wrong with folks trying to better their circumstances. But somewhere along the line, our relentless pursuit of possessions, status, and life-style has begun to overshadow all else.

Immense wealth, success, and celebrity are now glorified above all. Our aspirations are no longer shaped by the childhood friend who rises to the top of his field or the colleague who makes it to the executive suite. Now we look to the Beautiful People who grace magazine covers ~ the athletes, entertainers, entrepreneurs, and corporate deal-makers who become wealthy beyond anyone's wildest dreams.

Identity used to derive from your family, your community, and your personal values as expressed in word and deed. Now it seems to come mainly from what you own, what lifestyle you can flaunt, and what rung you occupy on the corporate ladder. Personal values have morphed into consumer and corporate values.

Affluence, pure and simple, has become the primary goal in life for mainstream Americans. In a 1970 UCLA study, nearly 80 percent of college freshmen said their purpose was to "discover a meaningful philosophy of life." When the same survey was repeated in 2005, three out of four said "being very well off financially" was their number-one aim.

The goal of "living a good life" now translates to "having the good life" ~ a distinction that seems to be made less and less often these days.

Everybody knows "you can't buy happiness," but that doesn't seem to stop us from trying. Time for simple pleasures evaporates as we work harder and longer in our quest for the bigger house, the more luxurious car, the more opulent lifestyle. American workers today put in more hours on the job than we did back in the 1950s, and on average we work nearly nine full weeks longer per year than our counterparts in Western Europe. No wonder we always seem to want more. We're so busy striving, we fail to realize that the things we crave don't bring us lasting satisfaction.

DAWSON

Winner Take All

Increasing economic competitiveness has only deepened our obsession with wealth. Those who make it to the top of the career ladder are doing better than ever ~ the average CEO salary more than tripled from 1993 to 2005 ~ while average Americans contend with mass layoffs, stagnant wages, and growing uncertainties over retirement. All too frequently, we see corporate honchos engineer leveraged buyouts that leave them set for life while they slash thousands of jobs in the name of "efficiency."

It's clear the game has changed. Instead of "play by the rules, share in the rewards," it's now more like "winner take all" ~ and those with wealth or position get to rewrite the rules when it serves their interests. Nobody who believes in free markets wants to begrudge rewards the rich and powerful have earned. After all, their success stories help fuel our own ambitions and drive. But we can't turn a blind eye when ordinary working families play by the rules only to end up living paycheck to paycheck ~ maybe even losing their livelihoods and security ~ just so some fat cats can further pad their portfolios.

In this country today, career success is no longer just something to strive for; it has become a matter of survival. If you don't make it to the top economic rung, you're going to be left behind ~ way behind. Even if you're hard-working, smart, and well-educated, there's no assurance you'll make the grade.

So it's no wonder that in our bottom-line society, kids are groomed from an early age to compete and win at any cost. Nor is it surprising that parents obsess over getting their toddlers into the right preschool. By seventh grade, kids are busy loading their transcripts with extra-curricular activities they think will appeal to college admission officers.

By the time high school graduation rolls around, anything less than a 4.0 GPA spells failure to students aiming for an Ivy League school. They know that with the right degree, college graduates can earn a six-figure salary right out the gate. Otherwise they may find themselves asking "Do you want fries with that?"

Of course there's rampant cheating in our schools and sharp-elbowed competitiveness in the workplace. With the pressures and stakes so high, people can justify almost anything to get ahead.

It's All About Me

When you look at the ways society has changed for the worse, the common thread is a growing self-absorption, if not out-and-out selfishness. Whoever coined the "Me Generation" had it wrong; we've become the "Me Nation." It's as though "What's in it for me?" has become our national motto. We all have to look out for our own interests, but our focus on "I, me, and mine" has gone way beyond that.

Back in the days when most of our population lived on farms or ranches, families were more isolated than today, yet far more interdependent. If the river flooded or you got too sick to bring in the crops, you'd look to your neighbors to help you pull through. You had to be part of the community to survive.

If I have a fault, it's probably that I'm far too modest about my many achievements!

DONALD TRUMP

During World War II, Americans planted victory gardens, lived with rationing of food, gas, clothes, and coffee, and observed a 35-mile-per-hour national speed limit ~ all to conserve resources for the war effort overseas. Historians tell us that some of these measures went beyond what was needed, but they were kept in place regardless. Why? Because our leaders believed it would boost civilian morale if we all made personal sacrifices for the greater good. Can you imagine that happening today?

Now we have every creature comfort and convenience at our disposal ~ yet somehow our lives feel empty. We're so preoccupied with the demands of career and household that many of us scarcely even know our neighbors, let alone feel a shared responsibility for their well-being. Small-town neighborliness still exists in rural pockets and in Disney movies. But the American Dream has morphed into a vision of secluded splendor ~ an upscale, gated community of suburban McMansions with a Lexus in every driveway and burglar alarms to safeguard the high-definition flat-screen plasma TVs.

Sure, we're busy. But the average household still finds time for eight hours and 14 minutes a day of TV, according to Nielsen research. It may be that the dramas and celebrities we watch help fill the void in our own lives. Hungry for meaningful interaction, millions of Americans devote leisure hours to linking up with others online. Isn't it ironic that we spend hours sitting alone in front of computers as we log onto social networking sites? We have become more connected than ever, yet less attached. More informed, but less in touch with the real world around us.

The more caught up we get in seeking personal comforts and gratification, the less inclined we are to give up anything for the general good. When a community-wide effort is needed or volunteers are called for, it's a whole lot easier to let someone else do the heavy lifting.

That's one reason we've become a nation governed by interest groups. No matter how worthy or widely embraced the goal ~ whether it be advancing toward energy independence, reining in health care costs, or simplifying the tax code ~

DAWSON

solutions become impossible if those with a vested interest have to give something up. We have become accustomed to always expecting more, never settling for less.

No one on their deathbed ever said: "My one regret is that I didn't spend more time alone with my computer."

A Nation Divided

Just as our lives suffer from the alienation between self and others, our country suffers from the widening breach between "us" and "them."

Whatever happened to the idea that we're all in this together?

These days, we seem to define ourselves by the things that divide us rather than the things we share. Too often we get a sense of our community by drawing lines around it.

Are we among the fortunate "haves," or the downtrodden "have-nots?" Racism has become politically incorrect, but class distinctions seem to endure stronger than ever. Are we members of the Business Roundtable, Sierra Club, or NRA? If so, that puts us in someone else's enemy camp. Do we belong to the Greatest Generation or the Hip-Hop Nation? The two speak a different language, if they speak at all.

Our country has lost the *shared values* ~ like fair play, self-reliance, and duty ~ that once united us and anchored our national identity. The more diverse we become in origins, culture, and lifestyle, the more we find ourselves at odds. So where do we get our shared values now? Some might say the Ten Commandments is not a bad place to start. I wouldn't argue with that; the trouble is, our country is as divided by religion as anything else.

Ever since the last presidential election, pundits have framed the big issues in terms of red states and blue states, but that's shorthand for a schism that has been growing for some time. Politically and culturally, we've become a nation polarized, with morality being the biggest battleground of all. On the one hand, we have the absolutists ~ those seeking to uphold traditional moral and religious structures above all else; on the other, the relativists ~ those who champion individual freedom and self-expression, letting the chips fall where they may.

To make matters worse, extremists from both camps have hijacked mainstream American values to further their own agendas. And so we find religion employed to preach intolerance and "family values" used to dictate what others can or cannot do. Meanwhile, others fly the banner of freedom to justify in-your-face behavior and anything-goes lifestyles, no matter how abhorrent they might be to the majority. Single-minded partisans on both sides have seized upon wedge issues, self-righteously exploiting them for political gain even as they talk about "uniting, rather than dividing." The rest of us are left struggling to find the middle ground where compromise and common-sense solutions may lie.

Politics is said to be the
second oldest profession.
I have come to realize that it bears
a very close resemblance to the first.

RONALD REAGAN

DAWSON

DAWSON

A Vacuum in Leadership

Throughout our history, we've looked to our leaders to express and embody American ideals. Think, for example, of Jefferson ("We hold these truths to be self-evident: that all men are created equal"); Lincoln ("As I would not be a slave, so I would not be a master"); Truman ("The buck stops here"); Kennedy ("Ask not what your country can do for you; ask what you can do for your country"); and Reagan ("Mr. Gorbachev, tear down this wall").

We still hear plenty of high-flown rhetoric from those who make and uphold our laws, but their actions speak louder. Lawmakers publicly condemn rampant waste and corruption while steering multi-million-dollar contracts to their cronies. The level of hypocrisy is staggering. If we assume that the influence-peddling indictments we've seen are just the tip of the iceberg, are we being churlish? Or merely realistic?

Where have all the real leaders gone? We desperately need men and women with the courage to buck constituents and campaign contributors when the broader national interest is at stake... independent thinkers who place their principles above party politics...true statesmen who continually remind us of the best things about our country and challenge us to live up to those standards.

Instead, our system of government is a cauldron of the same self-centeredness and ethics of convenience that are roiling the rest of our society. How do we teach grade-schoolers that "honesty is the best policy" when high officials are caught feeding the public convenient half-truths, if not out-and-out lies? Despite all the challenges we face as a nation, politicians have been afraid to ask the American people to face up to the hard realities and accept the necessary tradeoffs. Apparently they believe this generation isn't willing to give up anything for the sake of the next one. The question is, are they wrong?

Ninety percent of the politicians give the other ten percent a bad reputation.

HENRY KISSINGER

Why You Should Care

Think a few years or even decades down the road. What kind of world are we leaving our children and grandchildren? Do we really want them growing up to be as cynical as we have become? Looking back years from now, will we finally admit that we could have done something about global warming, but didn't want to take the financial hit? How will we feel watching future generations struggle under the mountain of debt we've bequeathed them in order to pay for our runaway spending today?

In our every deliberation, we must consider the impact of our decisions on the next seven generations.

THE GREAT LAW OF THE IROQUOIS CONFEDERACY

DAWSON

DAWSON

And what about your own legacy? Ask yourself, "How would I like to be remembered?" As "the top producer in the office" or "the one who came out on top in every business deal?" Or as someone who was an exceptional role model, a true friend, a person of substance and character?

If we hope to change things for the better, we need to build on what's best in America, and in ourselves. That's why stricter laws and more exhaustive ethical guidelines won't really help. There's always another way to get around them. Instead of more regulation, we need more inspiration ~ something beyond ourselves that will make us want to do better and be better than we are.

It's not how you're buried;

it's how they remember you.

JOHN WAYNE
in *The Cowboys*

What's the Cowboy Got to Do with It?

Throughout human history, we've always had heroes to remind us of our capacity for greatness. But if it's true that you can gauge a society by its heroes, it's easy to see why we're in trouble. Whom do we have to look up to these days? Political leaders? Sports figures? Corporate CEOs? People of the cloth? So many have let us down, shattering the esteem in which we once held them.

Today we have plenty of celebrities, but very few genuine heroes.

To my generation, cowboys were the biggest heroes of all, not just because they stood fearless in the face of danger, but because they were the good guys who held the line against evil and corruption. Devouring the Western novels of Louis L'Amour and the big-screen exploits of Roy Rogers and Gene Autry, my boyhood friends and I knew what we aspired to be. We wanted to grow up like the strong, steadfast men in the white hats ~ the ones who never hesitated to do what was right and could always be counted on in a pinch.

Half a century later, I've realized that cowboys are still my heroes. But instead of the iconic cowboys of story and screen, I now admire the real-life working cowboys and ranching families I've been lucky enough to meet. I can tell you there really *is* something special about genuine cowboys ~ and cowgirls, too. They carry themselves with an authenticity, a humbleness, and a kind of quiet confidence that leaves you with no doubt they are indeed "the real deal."

Of course, if you're not steeped in Western lore and life, you might think of the cowboy as quaint and irrelevant ~ a nostalgic footnote to American history. Worse still, the image of the cowboy has been cheapened and commercialized.

Ask today's typical urbanite about cowboys and the response will likely have something to do with gunslinging foreign policy, country music stars, or the Marlboro man.

What most people don't get is that being a cowboy isn't about the hat and boots. It's about choosing a simple, rugged way of life that's deeply connected to the land and the rhythms of nature. Even though family-owned ranches are rapidly dwindling, the Cowboy Way endures. All across the West, ranching families are still running herds and raising their children to a life of honest hard work. As I speak to audiences around the country, I constantly run across successful, well-educated people who attribute their achievements to the discipline and self-reliance they learned growing up on a ranch.

DAWSON

The Cowboy's Legacy

Being a cowboy also means living by a code ~ the Code of the West ~ that goes all the way back to the days of the open range. Back then, before the West was settled, there was no system of courts and laws. The cowboy code was the only civilizing authority. What's more, it had less to do with rules than with character and values like honesty, loyalty, and authenticity.

It's fascinating to note that the code was never set down in black-and-white; its tenets were unwritten and even unspoken. Yet every cowboy knew what they were. Doing such rough, dangerous work, cowboys had to know they could rely on the character of those who rode with them. Any cowboy who flouted the code quickly found himself shunned. Nobody had to ask if any laws had been broken. It was enough to know: "That ain't the Cowboy Way."

Of course, cowboying has changed a lot since the days of the big cattle drives 150 years ago. Today's ranch hands have cell phones and pickup trucks as well as saddles and spurs. But the core traditions remain intact. Cowboys still honor and live by their code. They are heroic because they stand for something ~ not just in word and belief, but in their actions each day.

When you think about it, the cowboy is the poster child for what you might call bedrock American values. Authentic working cowboys embody the *positive* qualities that built this country ~ values such as optimism, courage, hard work, and fair play. These traits are a big part of what makes us uniquely American.

If it's true you can't take it with you, then maybe it's about what you leave behind.

That's why the cowboy remains such a natural role model for our country today. Cowboy values are the ones all Americans can share, no matter what our religion, race, or politics, no matter whether we identify with red states or blue ones. They can help teach us how to live with heart and rebuild the tottering pillars of our society.

Cowboys have never been ones to leave behind great fortunes, grand buildings, or thriving enterprises. Typically, they owned little more than they could carry in their saddlebags.

The cowboy's code and quintessentially American values are his true legacy ~ a legacy we need to draw upon now if we want to restore America to greatness.

DAWSON

The CODE of the WEST

Ten Principles to Live By

1   LIVE EACH DAY WITH COURAGE

2   TAKE PRIDE IN YOUR WORK

3   ALWAYS FINISH WHAT YOU START

4   DO WHAT HAS TO BE DONE

5   BE TOUGH, BUT FAIR

6   WHEN YOU MAKE A PROMISE, KEEP IT

7   RIDE FOR THE BRAND

8   TALK LESS AND SAY MORE

9   REMEMBER THAT SOME THINGS AREN'T FOR SALE

10   KNOW WHERE TO DRAW THE LINE

from the book *"Cowboy Ethics: What Wall Street Can Learn from The Code of the West"*   ©2004 James P. Owen

MEHOSH

SEVEN CORE VALUES That Define America

These days, it's hard to say what America stands for. Yet I don't believe our country's idealism has been extinguished. A sense of higher purpose and the desire to live a meaningful life can still be found in the hearts, homes, and everyday lives of ordinary Americans all across the land.

What we've been missing is a reference point: a clear expression of the values all Americans can share no matter what our religion, origins, or politics. That's where the cowboy comes in. When you think about it, the cowboy's defining values are the same ones that built and, for many years, defined our country. Even today, the cowboy is a natural symbol of what's best about America. Take a good look at the images in these pages and you'll see why.

The Cowboy

Way

The spirit
of the cowboy
is the spirit
of America.

BECK

A person
must meet
fear to
know
courage.

COURAGE

With the cushioned, sanitized lives many Americans lead, we may not see *courage* as relevant to the everyday. It's a quality we hope we'll find in the drawer when and if we need it.

It's different for cowboys. The life of the saddle is a DAILY TEST of courage in all its forms ~ and there's no whining allowed, not ever.

How many of us risk life and limb in the regular course of our jobs each day? Every cowhand must be ready to face flying hooves, angry bulls, harsh conditions, and the other dangers that come with the territory.

But HEROISM need not involve high drama. Think of the sheer GRIT it takes to split fence rails in 110° heat or pursue a lost cow across miles of rugged terrain in sub-zero weather. Then there is MORAL COURAGE ~ the kind that calls for every effort and any sacrifice needed to uphold what is right.

For all their VALOR, cowboys never wear it on their sleeves.
They see courage as something to be taken for granted ~
a quality noticed only in its absence.

DAWSON

MOORHOUSE

CRISP

Courage

COURAGE GROWS FROM

- Acknowledging fear and confronting it head-on

- Accepting risk, change, and failure as part of life

- Persevering despite the odds

- Standing up for what we believe

- Enduring hardship and adversity without complaint

- Being willing to make the tough choices

- Living the life we want

The heroism of the working cowboy isn't a joke...it isn't something that has been cooked up by an advertising agency, and it isn't something that cheap minds will ever understand. Cowboys are heroic because they exercise human courage on a daily basis. They live with danger. They take chances. They sweat, they bleed, they burn in the summer and freeze in the winter. They find out how much a mere human can do, and then they do a little more. They reach beyond themselves.

JOHN R. ERICKSON

WHY WE NEED TO CULTIVATE **COURAGE**

Despite the comforts and conveniences that buffer us, our daily lives are still fraught with insecurity. We may not even be aware of the degree to which our actions are ruled by fear ~ fear of losing our jobs, of being judged by others, of harm that might befall us or our loved ones.

These fears can be paralyzing, keeping us from growing in experience and wisdom. They can also be corrosive. When we take the easy way out, rather than facing the challenge or making the tough choice, we only become weaker. This is true of societies as well as individuals.

Even if we are never called upon to brave a tsunami or rescue someone from a burning building, we all encounter situations that demand courage.

Success is not final, failure is not fatal. It is the courage to continue that counts.

WINSTON

CHURCHILL

Being a single parent, dealing with serious illness, telling difficult truths ~ all of us face these kinds of tests sooner or later. The more we learn to draw and rely upon our inner strength, the more our courage grows.

There ain't a horse
that can't be rode;
there ain't a cowboy
that can't be throwed.

COWBOY SAYING

Behold
the gift
of a
brand new
day.

OPTIMISM

Many of us use the word *optimism* in the sense of "expecting a favorable outcome." In cowboy country, it connotes something different.

Waking up each day to backbreaking work, often under hard conditions, cowboys need a CHEERFUL DISPOSITION just to exit their bunks. Seasoned hands operate with a quiet GOOD HUMOR that defies their clear-eyed grip on reality, for no one is more aware of how cruel and how random nature can be. The cowhand's brand of optimism isn't about believing things will go her way. It's about TAKING THINGS AS THEY COME, with the confidence that she can handle whatever happens. It's a POSITIVE OUTLOOK rooted in the rhythms of life. As long as we know the sun will rise on a new day tomorrow, there is HOPE FOR THE FUTURE.

BECK

PEACH

OPTIMISM GROWS FROM

- Faith in the rightness of the natural order of things

- Confidence in our own abilities

- Acceptance of the blending of good and bad in the world ~ and in ourselves

- Consciously choosing to focus on the good in our lives

- Gratitude for the blessings that come our way

Optimism

RYAN

Optimism is the faith

that leads to achievement.

Nothing can be done

without hope and confidence.

HELEN KELLER

WHY WE NEED TO CULTIVATE **OPTIMISM**

So much in our world is geared toward the negative, and our media culture only compounds the syndrome. Simply trying to keep up with world events means getting a constant barrage of input around themes of war, violence, crime, and turmoil.

In our own lives, we often focus on our problems and conflicts rather than on our advantages and good fortune. In fact, neuroscientists tell us that this bent toward adversity comes from our built-in survival mechanisms. The human autonomic nervous system is geared to detecting any potential threat and triggering an immediate "fight or flight" response.

This means we must make a conscious effort to take in the good, acknowledge it, and nurture it wherever and whenever we can.

It would be foolhardy to ignore genuine threats to our well-being and way of life, but both as individuals and as a society, we can only move forward if we believe in our potential to make things better.

Tomorrow is the most important thing in life. Comes into us at midnight very clean. It's perfect when it arrives and it puts itself in our hands. It hopes we've learned something from yesterday.

JOHN WAYNE

SELF-RELIANCE

The next time you need a mechanic or a doctor or a carpenter,
just imagine: What if you had to DO IT YOURSELF?

When you grow up the Cowboy Way, you learn *self-reliance* ~
to depend on your own SKILLS and PERSISTENCE
to get the job done ~ whatever it may be.

For cowboys, riding and roping is just the start.
Being able to mend a fence, cook a stew, fix an engine,
deliver a calf, or set a broken arm is a matter of pride
as well as necessity. They know the satisfaction of
MASTERY of a skill and the DIGNITY of doing
a job with their own two hands.

The cowboy's CAN-DO SPIRIT also
has deeper relevance to our times.
Each of us can do something to help fix
what's wrong with our country. Instead
of expecting government to step in,
maybe we should COUNT ON OURSELVES.

Always tighten
your own cinch.

If you're lookin' for a helpin' hand,

try the one on the end of your own damn arm.

COWBOY SAYING

Self-Reliance

VAN CLEVE

DUSARD

VAN CLEVE

SELF-RELIANCE GROWS FROM

- Taking responsibility for our own well-being

- Confidence in our ability to learn

- Making do with what we have

- Doing our best and learning from mistakes

- Valuing competence over convenience

- Putting in the time and effort it takes to master a skill

- Finding satisfaction in every accomplishment

**Do what needs doin';
scratch what needs scratchin'.**

COWBOY SAYING

In this country, we've taken the service economy to an extreme. Many Americans are tech-savvy and media-literate ~ but can't cook a simple meal, let alone fix what's broken around the house. We've become so pressed for time that we outsource even the most basic chores.

Over time, this pattern solidifies into a mindset of helplessness. The less we do for ourselves, the less we think we can do.

When it comes to big problems affecting us all, we simply assume someone else ~ the government or some nonprofit agency ~ will take care of it.

After Hurricane Katrina, how many scenes did we see of stranded, helpless people who had no idea of what to do next? A cowboy would never have just sat there, passively waiting for FEMA or the Red Cross to show up. He would have been busy figuring out how to get himself and everyone around him to safety. And if one way didn't work, he'd find another.

Think of the confidence ~ and competence ~ we could gain by following such an example.

*Figure out what
you stand for...
and what you won't.*

There's no mistaking a real cowboy. Even if you've never
set foot on a working ranch, you can still tell who's
"all hat and no cattle" and who's THE REAL DEAL.

An authentic cowboy carries himself with a quiet CONFIDENCE
that comes from knowing exactly who he is and what he's about.
Yet there's also a HUMBLENESS that shines through in his direct,
UNVARNISHED MANNER. He is proud without being prideful
and owns up to his shortcomings without hesitation.

The cowboy embodies the very meaning of INTEGRITY ~
that is, his actions line up with his beliefs. He inspires trust
and earns it by being TRUE TO HIMSELF and the cowboy code.

At a time when corporations, political candidates, and bloggers
turn themselves inside out to appear GENUINE, cowboys
know the secret: If you're HONEST in word, thought,
and deed, appearances will take care of themselves.

Cowboys may not have a monopoly on *authenticity*,
but few have done better at showing us what it means.

AUTHENTICITY

It ain't about the hat and boots.

BECK

KENDRICK

GUILDNER

GUILDNER

KENDRICK

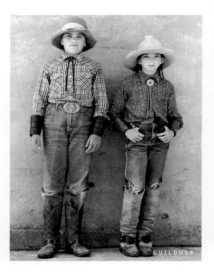

GUILDNER

KENDRICK

VAN CLEVE

KENDRICK

DERUYTTER

DUSARD

50

AUTHENTICITY GROWS FROM

- Understanding one's self as a whole person

- Satisfaction in being who we are

- Actions guided by a coherent set of core beliefs

- Recognizing our own strengths and weaknesses

- Saying what we mean

The rich man is not the one who has the most...but the one who needs the least.

Authenticity

MOORHOUSE

You never really know

the measure of a man

'til there's adversity

or money on the table.

WHY WE NEED TO CULTIVATE AUTHENTICITY

Our culture is obsessed with image. We are continually barraged with media messages that stoke our desires to be richer, better looking, and more successful. What's more, we measure that success based on outward appearances and tangible rewards. It's no wonder we sometimes fail to draw the distinction between self-creation ~ that is, deciding what kind of person we wish to be ~ and mere image-building.

This leads to unhappiness and conflict. For authenticity is not just an admirable trait, but a quality needed to get along in the world. Only when pretense, hypocrisy, and self-serving agendas are set aside can we approach life with understanding and compassion. By the same token, the more confident we feel in being who we genuinely are, the less likely we are to feel threatened by others. Aggression is fed by insecurity.

Authenticity is also essential to leadership. Only those who act out of inner conviction, rather than fear of failure, can risk making a tough call or striking out in new directions. It is this kind of confidence, especially in the face of adversity, that makes someone a leader others are willing to trust and follow.

Not surprisingly, the more rare we find authenticity to be, the higher the premium we place on people, places, and things that are genuine. We recognize the aura of truth when we see it.

52

Never cut what you can untie.

COWBOY SAYING

The word *honor* is rarely used these days, except in the sense of accolades or esteem publicly bestowed. But to a cowboy, being honorable is an inward, private matter that's as important as knowing how to ride and rope. If you are a man of honor, you are bound to DO THE RIGHT THING even ~ and especially ~ when no one is looking.

In the days of the open range, when homesteads were far from any civilizing influence, this view of honor was a practical necessity. It was up to each man to UPHOLD VIRTUE and STAND SQUARE against evil, starting with his own conduct.

Modern-day cowboys still use their own MORAL COMPASS to determine what is right and what is wrong. They know that laws and rules, which can always be bent, are no substitute for PERSONAL INTEGRITY. For them, CHARACTER counts above all.

A man who would die for something has everything to live for.

HONOR

DAWSON

Honor

HONOR MEANS

- Being worthy of trust

- Someone who can be counted on

- Telling the truth

- Keeping our word

- Acting with integrity, no matter the cost

- Knowing that just because it's legal doesn't mean it's right

56

SERPA

VAN CLEVE

The best sermons are lived,

not preached.

WHY WE NEED TO CULTIVATE A SENSE OF **HONOR**

We live in cynical and morally confusing times. Transgressions on the order of academic cheating and dishonest business dealings are increasingly shrugged off on the basis that "everybody does it" or "it's no big deal." We also see public figures getting away with ~ even flaunting ~ more serious misdeeds, so long as they can afford the right legal talent.

Our society is so obsessed with "self" and success that we've already tumbled down some morally slippery slopes. "The end justifies the means" has become an unspoken operating principle ~ one so pervasive that many Americans assume you can't get ahead if you're not willing to break the rules.

Being a person of honor is the way to a more meaningful, satisfying life, regardless of society's failings. We gain self-respect by setting our own standards and holding ourselves accountable to them. We gain clarity and confidence by knowing which lines we will not cross. And we gain nobility by paying heed to principles larger than ourselves. Those who live with honor are the backbone of our society and the ones who ultimately reap life's richest rewards.

CRISP

Since ancient times, philosophers have debated the kinds of MORAL OBLIGATIONS that should override self-interest and lead us to appropriate action. A cowboy would put it more plainly: He has to look out for the herd and the ranch no matter what. Without question or complaint, he puts *duty* first. Why else would someone go out into a blizzard to rescue a calf that may not even belong to him?

Of course, the cowboy's SENSE OF RESPONSIBILITY extends far beyond his job, embracing larger ideals. His Old West tradition was forged at a time when brave, right-minded men were the only bulwark against the dangers and lawlessness of the frontier.

Men and women of the saddle still take that role to heart ~ standing ready to HELP and PROTECT when family, community, or country might be in need. They are no less obliged to intervene when principles such as freedom or justice are at stake. Being a cowboy means you are BOUND BY YOUR CODE.

DUTY

Never say "Whoa" in a tight spot.

DAWSON

PEACH

RYAN

PEACH

MEHOSH

DERUYTTER

DUTY MEANS

- Actions, not words

- Responsibility to something larger than one's self

- A willingness to sacrifice self-interest

- Doing what has to be done

- Respecting core values as absolutes

- Answering the call when it comes

Duty

62

If you open the gate, close it.

If you didn't open it,

close it anyway.

COWBOY SAYING

WHY WE NEED TO CULTIVATE A SENSE OF **DUTY**

MEHOSH

VAN CLEVE

America has always been a place where the freedom of individuals is held dear. What other country declares the "pursuit of happiness" to be an inalienable right, as stated in our Declaration of Independence?

In years past, families, schools, and other institutions strived to produce citizens who understood that freedom cannot be separated from its flip side ~ responsibility to others. Values such as civility, generosity, and love of country were seen as a necessary balance to personal ambition and achievement.

More recently, however, the balance has shifted. The focus on "self" and the drive for economic and social success have intensified to the point where there is no stigma in neglecting obligations to others; it's simply assumed that "someone else" will take care of it.

When idealism and self-sacrifice are seen as obsolete notions, it's high time for the pendulum to swing back.

MOORHOUSE

"Pard, you'll do to ride the river with," is the highest compliment a cowboy can pay.

A heart knows things a head never will.

HEART

Difficult to define, yet unmistakable when present, *heart* is the quality that enfolds all other values. A generous impulse, an encouraging word, a random act of kindness, a tender thought ~ heart finds expression in a thousand ways.

Heart means being OPEN TO UNDERSTANDING and ACCEPTANCE OF OTHERS. It reaches out to find CONNECTION with humanity and the natural world. It is that readiness to give that comes from SELFLESSNESS. Heart embraces the TRUTH and finds JOY, even among thorns.

Fixated on the quantifiable and material, our culture often mistrusts what can't be neatly defined. Americans tend to relegate heart to certain domains ~ family, charitable endeavors, the helping professions ~ separate from practical concerns. But when we push heart away, we rob ourselves of WHOLENESS and daily life of its richness.

Cowboys show us a more complete way of being. Tough but COMPASSIONATE, they are caretakers, guardians, and helpers at the core. Ultimately, heart is what being a cowboy is all about.

PEACH

SERPA

MEHOSH

CRISP

PEACH

HEART IS ABOUT

- Seeing the good in people

- Seeing the beauty in life

- Finding rewards in giving

- Recognizing our shared humanity

- Feeling at one with nature

- Kindness to all living creatures ~ including ourselves

Heart

CRISP (series of five)

MOORHOUSE

CRISP

PEACH

The shortest distance

between two points

is riding with

a good friend.

CRISP

MOORHOUSE

A cowboy knows
that the best things
in life aren't things.

VAN CLEVE

PEACH

WHAT WILL I TELL HIM?

BY WADDIE MITCHELL
COWBOY POET

What will I tell him, you ask me,
When my son's trying to make up his mind?
To ride for a living like I have,
Or explore what the world has to find?
Could I tell him it's sure worth the doing?
Could I tell him I spent well my time?
I'll just say from the start,
Son, it's gotta come from the heart;
It ain't something that comes from the mind.

I'll tell him the truth as I know it ~
Of good years, hard winters, and drought.
The ecstasy of winning a round now and then,
Givin' courage to stay in the bout.
That adrenaline rush when you're bustin' up brush
On a cowpony, agile and stout,

Of havin' the rug jerked from under your feet
When you hear that the outfit's sold out.

I'll tell him that cowboy's a verb, not a noun:
It's what you do more than a name.
And he'd be foolin' himself if he's figurin' on
Any sort of material gain.
I'll remind him of spring calves a-buckin'.
Of the joy and the pride and the pain
Of livin' a life that is easy or hard
At the discretion of nature's refrain.

What will I tell him, you ask me,
When he's there and tryin' to make up his mind?
I'll just say from the start,
Son, it's gotta come from the heart;
It ain't something that comes from the mind.

SERPA

A true friend is someone who reaches for your hand and touches your heart.

WHY WE NEED TO CULTIVATE **HEART**

We live in an increasingly bottom-line society ~ one in which human dimensions are too often neglected or outweighed by matters of profit or convenience. If you think that's too harsh an assessment, consider the disgraceful aftermath of Hurricane Katrina...or the shameful treatment of our veterans...or our chronic failure to ease the plight of the homeless or the medically uninsured. It's hard not to believe that heart is a shrinking element of our national character.

America is resented not just because we are the richest and most powerful country in the world, but because our national priorities are out of whack. Our leaders act out of self-interest, ideology, party loyalty ~ anything but heart. To change that, we must do more than pay lip service to humanitarian ideals. We can shift the balance ~ but only if we learn to live with heart.

You don't have to be a cowboy to live with heart. You might be a single mom working two jobs who always finds time to help with homework. Or someone who puts a career on hold to care for an aging parent. Or the businessman who cuts his own salary to keep from laying off loyal workers.

If we can make heart the core of our lives, America will surely regain what she has lost.

BECK

we can all share

1 COURAGE

2 OPTIMISM

3 SELF-RELIANCE

4 AUTHENTICITY

5 HONOR

6 DUTY

7 HEART

DAWSON

BECK

Recapturing what

America once stood for

WHAT DOES IT MEAN TO BE AN AMERICAN?

THESE ARE TIMES OF SOUL-SEARCHING for our country, and rightly so. With our nation facing so many thorny problems and seemingly intractable policy stalemates, the questions that framed our high school civics classes now have fresh relevance. What does it mean to be an American today? Just what is it that characterizes our increasingly diverse nation? And what role should each of us play in advancing this idea of America?

Ask members of the cultural elite ~ the leading lights of this nation's op-ed pages, blogs, and Sunday morning talk shows ~ and you'll get any number of interpretations of what America stands for. Depending on which thinker or pundit you turn to, you might hear that America is about egalitarianism, or "exceptionalism," or innovation, or enlightened self-interest, or global stewardship, or sovereignty of the people, or even self-righteous imperialism.

But if you take the nation's pulse by talking with groups of ordinary Americans, as I've had the chance to do, you'll find the popular notion of America hasn't changed much since the days of Tom Paine and Thomas Jefferson.

For most of us, being an American is still about having the personal freedom to pursue our dreams, whatever they may be. Just ask those who have pulled themselves up from poverty through business, law, or medical school, or the immigrants who have risked their lives to reach our shores, or the entrepreneurs who turned an idea, a little bit of capital, and a lot of sweat into a thriving corporation.

CRISP

80

DAWSON

DAWSON

A Generation Blessed

No generation has benefited more from this climate of opportunity than the post-war Baby Boomers who are now beginning to reach retirement age. (Full disclosure here: Although my birth certificate shows that I somewhat pre-date the Baby Boom generation, I consider myself an honorary member by virtue of the amount of hair I still have.)

Not only have we benefited from a huge transfer of wealth from our parents, we have had decades of peace, economic expansion, and bull markets in which to raise our families and make our fortunes. This isn't to say that the good life was just handed to us. But those of us who got an education and were willing to work hard generally found success within our reach. Judging by the enormous affluence so visible all around us today, many in this generation achieved more than our parents could ever have imagined.

To a large extent, prosperity has liberated us to choose the kind of life we want to lead, which is another dimension of freedom. Millions have been able to live in comfortable homes and safe, attractive communities, give our children a good start in life, and enjoy the many pleasures available to us.

So why do so many of us find personal fulfillment so elusive?

If we're fortunate, as we get older we learn what philosophers and Hollywood movies have repeatedly told us: Happiness doesn't come from the career success we achieve, the status we enjoy, or the material things we accumulate. It comes from living with heart. That's the kind of wisdom they don't teach in business school.

In his 2006 book, *Stumbling on Happiness*, Harvard psychologist Daniel Gilbert asks a simple question: What would you do if you knew you were going to die in ten minutes? As he notes, it's "hard to say, of course, but of all the things you might do in your final ten minutes, it's a pretty safe bet that

83

few of them are things you actually did today." His question is an invitation to think about what really matters to us ~ and if we're honest with ourselves, it's probably not a faster car or a more impressive job title.

Baby Boomers who devoted their earlier years to career-building now have the chance to do something else ~ to embark on other kinds of endeavors that have the potential to bring greater meaning and more lasting satisfaction to their lives. The idea that "there are no second acts in American lives" has become obsolete. As members of this generation re-invent the concept of retirement, they have the opportunity to find and follow new passions in life. And the more they do so, the greater the possibility they can exert real leadership and be a force for positive change in the world.

Intertwined with this opportunity is a strong sense of obligation. Having been the recipients of such enormous economic and demographic good fortune, Baby Boomers have an implicit responsibility to those who have been left behind through accidents of birth or geography. After all, hasn't America's greatness rested in part on its willingness to step in and liberate the oppressed, defend the downtrodden, and aid the afflicted all around the world? Even though our government hasn't always stepped up to the plate ~ Rwanda and Darfur spring to mind ~ the American people are justly known for their outpourings of generosity toward those in need.

Idealism is a big part of what it means to be an American.

Once we commit to the idea that we are all obliged to help make the world a better place ~ to make some contribution proportional to all we have received ~ we bump right up against the question *"What can I do?"*

***Think of "giving back"
as the rent you pay
for living on this planet.***

DERUYTTER

The Power of One

One of the maladies of our times is the feeling of gloom that pervades America's public life. As satisfied and optimistic as we individually may be concerning our private lives, polls show we are unrelentingly glum about our collective future and cynical about our public institutions. Our leaders seem paralyzed in the grip of a host of problems, from global warming, immigration, and health care to Social Security, poverty, and international terrorism, to name just a few. And when we see such dismal responses as the Hurricane Katrina debacle or the shoddy treatment of veterans wounded in Iraq, gloom turns to hopelessness.

Is this really the best we can do?

While nearly two-thirds of Americans say they are satisfied with their lives overall, only 25 percent are satisfied with the state of the nation, according to the Pew Research Center. But what if we start to think of this "happiness gap" as fertile ground for nurturing new, socially conscious ideas and ventures?

Powerless as we might feel to do anything about the folly in Iraq or our mounting national debt, that shouldn't keep us from being a positive force ~ in fact, it could even ignite our resolve. With a little creativity and a commitment to do *something*, each of us can find some way to make a difference, however modest. The retiree who tutors inner-city kids...the dentist who does an annual stint at a free clinic in Guatemala...the high school student who volunteers a day each month at a community soup kitchen. The possibilities are limitless.

Of course, we can always write a check; nonprofits need cash as well as volunteers. But when we get involved in a personal, hands-on way, it sets up a completely different dynamic: one in which whatever time and energy we give yields a rich dividend in terms of the satisfaction and expanded awareness we get back.

We make a living by what we get;
we make a life by what we give.

WINSTON CHURCHILL

DAWSON

87

MOORHOUSE

A Personal Journey

I have to admit that it took me a while to figure out what I could do. Having spent most of my career as a Wall Street "rainmaker," I wasn't sure how my skills would translate. But one day, I was struck by an inspiration. Discouraged by the evident breakdown of business ethics in our country, and dismayed by our increasingly crass, materialistic culture, I thought back to the cowboy heroes of my childhood.

It was then I realized that the matinee idols of my youth had been a huge influence on my thinking and values. It wasn't just because my cowboy heroes were strong and brave, but because they were unwavering in the principles of honor, loyalty, and courage they lived by each day. For them, it wasn't about rules or "ethics." It was about character and doing the right thing, no matter what.

Wouldn't America be a better place, I thought, if we all had a code to live by?

For me, this opened the door to a new passion ~ some might call it an obsession ~ in my life. I began seriously researching cowboy literature and lore. My evenings were spent revisiting classic Western movies such as *Red River, High Noon,* and *Shane*, as well as more recent masterpieces of the genre, including *Monte Walsh*, *Lonesome Dove,* and *Open Range*. I also spent time with real-life cowboys on modern-day working ranches and found that the important things haven't changed. Today's cowboys still honor and live by their code.

As I started sharing my thoughts with friends and colleagues, I found that many of them felt much the same way I did, only they hadn't quite put it into words yet.

Suddenly it all became clear. This is what *I* could do! Throughout my career, writing and speaking have always been my forte. Only now, rather than writing or giving speeches about investing, I talk about cowboys as a way to get people thinking about their own values and the values that define our country.

Sure, it was nerve-wracking the first time I got up before an audience to say in public what I had been thinking in private. And believe me, I've taken my share of ridicule from hard-nosed folks who believe the almighty dollar overrides all else. But when I hear from readers who say my take on America's shared values strikes a chord with them, or businesspeople who want to buy copies of my book for their clients, or teachers who are using *Cowboy Ethics* in their classrooms ~ well, I can only say that it's given me more real satisfaction than anything else I've ever done.

I'd figured that at this point in my life I'd be settled into a comfortable, leisurely retirement. That thought has vanished. Golf can wait. This is where I'm putting my energy now.

DAWSON

89

Finding New Passions

I've described my personal epiphany not because I think it's so unusual or special, but because I believe this kind of experience is becoming increasingly common. As fixated on wealth and self-gratification as our country has become, I'm convinced the pendulum has already begun to swing back. Americans are hungry for more meaning in their lives. What's more, I believe many are finding it ~ or will, as they grow older and have the chance to gain new perspective on their lives.

Let's be realistic. In our competitive economy, it takes enormous focus, energy, and determination to be successful. Even those who are blessed with above-average intelligence and talent must work hard to make the most of those gifts. That means that through our twenties, thirties, and even into our forties and fifties, many of us are so busy striving to build a business or a career that we're hard-pressed to make time for family life, let alone much else.

But if we learn to listen to the voices within, and not just the drumbeat of the workplace, we eventually reach the point where we realize there's a lot more to life than financial success. It might happen with a major disruptive life event, such as a divorce or business reversal. Or when an illness, disability, or the death of someone close to us puts us face-to-face with mortality. It can even come to those who finally get the big career payoff they have been pursuing, only to find it's not the be-all and end-all they had imagined.

Then, perhaps for the first time, we are ready to look beyond our youthful ambitions and examine what is truly important. What kind of life do we really want to lead? What else can we do with our God-given talents? And what kind of world do we want to leave behind for our children and grandchildren?

In short, this is when we can finally make room for heart in our lives.

For women, so many of whom work hard at balancing career with family and friends throughout their adult lives, this may not be such a great leap. Researchers have found that females are not only culturally encouraged, but genetically wired to nurture and relate to others.

On the other hand, this life passage can seem threatening to men, whose lives are often spent in settings where any display of heart or emotion is taken as a sign of weakness. But as one who has been through this metamorphosis, I promise that it can be immensely liberating. A reconstructed careerist who unexpectedly found his way to a more heart-centered way of life, I can attest to the rush of freedom that came from opening up previously hidden parts of myself.

One thing I know for sure: Now that I've crossed that threshold, I'll never go back.

A Process of Discovery

Where "living with heart" begins depends on each individual. For some, it starts with discovering new ways to use their gifts in the context of "us" and not just "me."

Each of us has some talent or skill we can apply, some contribution we can make. Such endeavors can range from traditional kinds of community or public service to creative and even pioneering forms of social entrepreneurship. I'm convinced that the most effective and innovative approaches to problems such as illiteracy or homelessness or global warming will not come from bureaucrats, but from talented individuals who have decided to care deeply about something and dedicate themselves to it.

Throughout America's history, the blending of individual enterprise with collective purpose has been one of our greatest strengths. That is how we went from being colonies to creating a country, how we settled the West, and how we grew to become the world's leading democratic society. It's a strength we need now more than ever.

Of course, living with heart can also arise from the everyday. Recently I visited with a longtime business acquaintance who had been such a formidable and commanding presence in the company he headed that he would literally make junior executives quake. Right up until the day he passed the baton to his successor, he was known for being as ruthless as he was brilliant.

Now, sitting with him in his lush garden on a warm Santa Barbara afternoon, I barely recognized this silver-haired, patrician-looking gentleman who positively glowed as he spoke of his granddaughter's medals for competitive swimming and showed me the roses he lovingly tended. "Aren't we lucky to be sitting here in this glorious spot?" he remarked, turning his beaming face toward the sun. Then he turned to me and said with just a tinge of regret, "You know, I lived here for years and never really saw it."

Nothing more needed to be said. He had been reborn into a new and more satisfying way of looking at the world, and we both understood how that was a kind of miracle.

The power of heart is that no matter where it takes root, it starts putting out shoots in all directions. Living with heart connects us with the world in new and often surprising ways. It becomes a way of being that opens us up to our kinship with the rest of humanity, our place in nature, and the fullness of our own experiences. It does not demand grand gestures or exhaustive efforts. It simply asks us to pay attention as whole beings ready to embrace what is good in life.

Be the change

that you want to see

in the world.

GANDHI

BECK

A Hopeful View

It is in the rich soil of heart-centered individual lives that qualities such as optimism, honor, and self-respect can flourish. Americans used to take pride in these ingredients of our national character. I hope we will again.

Please understand that I am not advocating nostalgia as an answer to tough issues, nor am I pitching some utopian vision of our future. Today's world is complex, and becoming more so all the time.

But to me, that's all the more reason why we need to reclaim the idealism and the shared values upon which our country was built. Harking back to what's good about our nation can give us the conviction we need to move forward.

I also believe that we haven't lost our capacity for greatness so much as lost sight of it. The qualities that made America great are still there at the core ~ still residing in our national DNA amid all the chaos, fear, and uncertainty roiling our country today. As we face our many problems, we need to remind ourselves that Americans still have a lot of things to be proud of, our legacy of shared values being one of them.

If each one of us becomes a force for the common good, and we see others doing the same, just think how powerful that can be. The impact of this movement won't come from the kinds of dramatic success stories it takes to rate a spot on Oprah's couch. It will come from the accumulation of many small contributions made by individual Americans all across the land.

In his best-seller, *The Tipping Point*, journalist Malcolm Gladwell shows how small shifts in behavior on the part of a few people can end up having a big effect as ideas spread "virally" and take hold. I know it will take a groundswell of change to heal what ails our country, and we'll need fresh thinking and new resolve to make it happen. But we do have reasons for hope.

After all, America's future has never depended on its leaders. Our country's strength has always been in its people ~ the everyday heroes who get up, go to work each day, and show by their actions what it means to live with heart. It is they ~ not the intellectuals, the politicians, or the power brokers ~ who are the true keepers of American ideals and values.

When I see real people whose lives embody the best qualities of America, I am more optimistic than ever. If we let ourselves be guided by the realization that we are all in this together, I believe we can move toward a society where honor is more fashionable than irony and character counts for more than celebrity.

I like to think America's best days lie ahead.

*I like to think
America's best days
lie ahead.*

THE COLLABORATORS

The Core Team

This book grew from a kind of collaboration few people are ever fortunate enough to experience. For more than a year, the three of us worked together in what can only be described as an extended and intense creative conversation. **Jim Owen** was the initiator and content driver ~ the man with a message and a singular vision. **Brigitte LeBlanc** not only helped translate Jim's ideas into structure and prose, but also ran with them, discovering new connections and inspirations in sometimes unexpected places. **Nita Alvarez** pored over several thousand photographs to find the perfect images and, ably assisted by the meticulous **Connie Broussard**, brought the team's vision to life as a rich tapestry of words and visuals. True to her nature, Nita also played the roles of muse and creative midwife throughout. What we do together, we could never hope to achieve individually; nor does any of us experience the same dynamic in any other context. Our collective output always seems to transcend the sum of its parts, which may be the best way to define true collaboration.

Having worked together on a score of large and small projects over the past 15 years, we have learned that a partnership like ours can't be programmed or forced; it can only be nurtured. Sometimes, magic happens ~ and we are as surprised by it as anyone else.

The Artists

The photographers represented in these pages were also partners in shaping this book. Not only was their work an abiding source of inspiration, they were active participants in giving our ideas visual expression. We are confident in saying that those who contributed did so because they believed in the book's message. Otherwise, they would not have spent so many hours sifting their archives for the photographs that best express what cowboy values are all about. Since we cannot possibly give our contributors their due in this limited space, we have posted capsule bios, sample images, and contact information for each artist at **www.cowboyethics.org**. We encourage you to visit the Center for Cowboy Ethics and Leadership website to learn more about the wonderful Western artists listed on the following pages.

Support and Inspiration

We are grateful to **Maureen Graney**, Editor-in-Chief, The Lyons Press, for her unflagging enthusiasm and support. This book was our team's first project with Maureen, and she proved to be an ideal editor and guide. From the outset, she understood and bought into our vision. As the book evolved, she stepped in with a sure and expert hand whenever an outside perspective was needed. The rest of the time, she stepped back, trusting the team's creative process and giving it the room it needed to unfold.

Three people connected with the Center for Cowboy Ethics and Leadership deserve special mention. **GB Oliver III**, a Director of the Center and its Resident Cowboy, was a major source of inspiration and our "go-to guy" for all questions concerning cowboy authenticity. A rancher, bronc buster, and storyteller ~ in short, a cowboy's cowboy ~ GB is a living example of cowboy values in action. He was also pressed into service, albeit reluctantly, as the model for the book's cover photo. As a friend and as Executive Director of the Paragon Foundation, where the Center is housed, GB helped the project in innumerable ways. **Nicole Krebs**, Deputy Director for the Center, kept us going with her infectious cowgirl spirit as she handled the myriad details that go along with any project of this scope. Thanks are also due to **Bill Reynolds**, another Director of the Center and Editor-in-Chief of *Living Cowboy Ethics*, the quarterly publication of the Paragon Foundation. Not only did Bill give us the benefit of his distinguished publishing background, he was a resource and sounding board for ideas.

Jim's partners and colleagues at Austin Capital Management ~ particularly **Chuck Riley**, **Brent Martin**, and **David Friedman** ~ deserve special mention. Without their support, this book would never have become a reality. **Beth Perl** very graciously offered her incisive commentary at many points throughout.

All royalties from this book go to support the activities of The Center for Cowboy Ethics and Leadership. To learn more, please visit www.cowboyethics.org.

THE ARTISTS

MYRON BECK is a leading Southern California–based advertising photographer, who specializes in people, animals, and lifestyles. He also acts as director of photography on live-action shoots for national clients. Myron's personal project for the last 20 years has been documenting the life of a traditional ranch family which embodies Western ethics, values, and morals. He has made more than 50 trips to the ranch in Zion, Utah, with the goal of producing a documentary book and film.

DIANE BOHNA CRISP was raised on a fifth-generation cattle ranch and follows the cowboy code. She has dedicated herself to preserving the American cowboy through camera lenses as well as her ranching way of life. A traditionalist in style, she specializes in riding and working with her proud subjects in order to capture the essence of cowboy soul. Diane is also an accomplished storyteller who shares her rich, poignant, and humorous tales of life on the land with audiences young and old.

ROBERT DAWSON began his romance with the West growing up in Texas. He has published four books and is producing a line of posters and greeting cards, as well as a series of fine art tapestries with Pendleton Woolen Mills. Robert's donations of photographic prints raised over $15,000 in 2006 for the "Agriculture in the Classroom" program. In 2007, he donated over $4,500 of his work in partnership with Primedia Publishing to "Riding for the Children," a benefit for the Linsenhoff UNICEF Foundation.

WOUTER DERUYTTER, noted Belgian photographer, currently lives and works in New York. Having spent much of his career capturing images of vanishing and fading cultures around the world, he is especially known for his photographs of people in the masks and costumes of their identities. In 1997, his attention turned to the American West. The result was published in his book, *Cowboy Code*. Wouter's work has been exhibited extensively in museums and galleries worldwide.

JAY DUSARD was awarded a 1981 Guggenheim Fellowship in Photography and has won two book awards. Having studied with Ansel Adams and Frederick Sommer, he is recognized as a consummate creator of images, and one of the greatest black-and-white printmakers. Now living in Arizona, Jay is best known for his images of the cowboy and American West. His books include *The North American Cowboy: A Portrait* and *Open Country*. He has conducted photography workshops for 30 years.

MEHOSH DZIADZIO grew up in New York and learned photography by assisting some of the city's top commercial photographers. Now based in beautiful Santa Barbara, California, he maintains a national presence by shooting advertising and editorial images that appear in national and international catalogs and magazines for a diverse group of clients. With over 30 years of experience, much of his inspiration is drawn from his love of the outdoors and the cowboy way of life.

CW GUILDNER is a native Nebraskan who began photographing the landscape and the lives of people in the rural heartland in 1990. This project evolved into an ongoing quest to record and express his vision of the many "Lives of Tradition" he finds as he travels across the United States. Since 2002, CW has been building a body of work around his interest in the vanishing "rural schoolhouse." He has visited over 4o of these remote schools to date as he documents this still-existing culture.

ROBB KENDRICK is an award-winning photographer whose work appears in major publications such as *National Geographic*. He is highly acclaimed for his art photos made on metal plates called tintypes, which are sought after by collectors and have been compiled in the celebrated book, *Revealing Character*. A second book of cowboy tintypes, *Still: Cowboys at the Start of the Twenty-First Century,* was published by University of Texas Press in January 2008. He resides in San Miguel de Allende, Mexico, with his family.

100

DIANE LACY is a freelance Western artist and award-winning photographer from Fort Davis, Texas. Her work has been featured in newspapers, magazines, and books and can be found in collections around the world. Diane chairs and is the writer for the DMTPHA, a project that publishes "Conservation Roundup," which is distributed free to schools to better educate young people about ranch life, land, and wildlife management, and to maintain a vital interest in the future of the livestock industry.

LOUISE SERPA is an accomplished photographer, whose 45 years of rodeo images capture the sport's energy and emotion. Dubbed the "Ansel Adams of the sport," this New York socialite moved out west and turned her hobby into a career in the 60s. She was the first woman allowed in the rodeo arena in 1963 and the first woman on the Course of the Grand National Steeple Chase in the UK in 1970. She was inducted into the Cowgirl Hall of Fame in 2000. Her book, *Rodeo*, includes commentary by Larry McMurtry.

BOB MOORHOUSE has chronicled the cowboy way of life for more than 20 years. Until his recent retirement, he served as Vice-President and General Manager of the Pitchfork Land and Cattle Company in Texas and Kansas. For 35 years, that role gave him the inspiration and the opportunity to create a huge collection of photographic art, some of which was published in *Pitchfork Country: The Photography of Bob Moorhouse*. Bob was inducted into the Texas Cowboy Hall of Fame in 2002.

BARBARA VAN CLEVE was born on her family's Montana ranch, which was founded in 1880, and began photographing her world at age 11. She has had over 51 one-person shows and nearly 75 group shows. Her work is collected internationally, and has been published in a number of books, including her own *Hard Twist: Western Ranch Women*. The subject of a 30-minute video documentary, "Barbara Van Cleve: Capturing Grace" in 1993, she has also been inducted into the Cowgirl Hall of Fame.

GENE PEACH has been photographing the cultures of the West for more than 20 years. His Southwestern, American Indian, and cowboy photos are published internationally, and his advertising and editorial photography appears regularly in U.S. magazines and books. His award-winning book about ranch and rodeo children, *Making a Hand: Growing up Cowboy in New Mexico*, will be followed by a volume on elderly Southern farmers titled *Difficult and Defeated, Tennessee*.

JAMIE WILLIAMS has been a commercial photographer for over 20 years. A native Texan now based in Tucson, she works with a diverse range of clients and national publications. She is also a filmmaker. In 2006, Jamie received an Artists Projects grant from the Arizona Commission on the Arts for her current endeavor: "American Cowgirl," a multimedia documentary that honors the women who shaped the American West and who continue to keep that spirit alive.

KATHLEEN JO RYAN is an award-winning photographer, multimedia producer, and filmmaker whose first love is the American West. She has sold over 125,000 copies of her five lavish photographic books, had four one-woman photographic exhibitions, and produced nationally televised documentaries. She and her brother, John, were recently honored for their outstanding documentary, "Right to Risk." It chronicles eight individuals with disabilities on a Grand Canyon whitewater rafting adventure.

WADDIE MITCHELL was named "America's best-known cowboy poet" by *People* magazine. A working cowboy from Nebraska, he has performed around the world, made numerous television appearances, been featured in newspapers, magazines, and books, and won critical acclaim for his many recordings for Western Jubilee Recording Co. Waddie founded the Working Ranch Cowboy Association to create scholarships and crisis funds for working cowboys and their families.

DAWSON

anaging Director of Austin Capital Management, an affiliate of Victory Capital Management.
d President of the Center for Cowboy Ethics and Leadership and author of the book *Cowboy*
eet Can Learn from the Code of the West. Jim's Wall Street career has spanned 40 years,
ner with NWQ Investment Management Company in Los Angeles. He is co-founder and Chair-
nent Management Consultants Association (IMCA). Profiled in the *Wall Street Journal* as a lead-
Jim has also been a prolific speaker and author. His book credits include *The Prudent Investor's*
ting from Uncertainty and Volatility (John Wiley & Sons, 2000) and *The Prudent Investor: The*
nal Investment Management (McGraw-Hill, 1990).

sh of corporate scandals and growing societal discord, Jim launched a second career as a so-
 ways to strengthen the foundation of shared values in American society. Inspired by his life-
tory and lore, Jim coined the phrase "cowboy ethics" and wrote his book distilling the Code
ples to Live By." To date, some 70,000 copies of the book have been sold.

raduate of Regis University. He is a past President of the Board of Trustees of the Santa Bar-
and his wife, Stanya, are the proud parents of two grown children, Win and Allegra.
me in Austin, Texas.

.cowboyethics.org.